PASCAL'S BASIC PRIMARY

spelling

How to become a good speller

by P Walker

LOOK INSIDE!

How to use this book...

Pascal's Basic Primary Spelling has been designed to teach you **how** to spell. Beginning with the basic letter/sound relationships, it moves step-by-step through to longer and more difficult words. This book is meant to be worked through from **beginning to end.**

To get the most out of this book, take the time to understand what each page is asking you to do. If you get stuck on one question, move on, and then come back and try again. If you still can't do it, look at the answer and then try some of the others.

Reviews are included so that you can check your progress. Skim through the work you have done before you attempt these reviews.

Remember, this book is designed to make learning to spell fun, so if you get tired or frustrated – take a break.

CONTENTS

Sounds & Blends

Look at these words and sound out the first letter.

<u>t</u>en **10** has the sound 'te'.

<u>b</u>at

<u>h</u>ut

<u>k</u>ite

<u>f</u>an

<u>t</u>in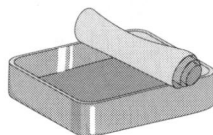

<u>p</u>ig

<u>j</u>ar

<u>w</u>all

<u>s</u>un

<u>l</u>eg

match

dog

cat

orange

van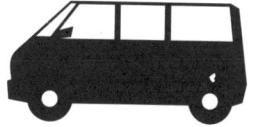

rat

nut

zipper

yell

axe

gun

egg

ink

umbrella

INITIAL BLENDS

Look at each word and sound out the first two letters.

<u>st</u>ick  has the sound 'ste'.

<u>fl</u>y

<u>fr</u>og

<u>dr</u>um

<u>sl</u>eep

<u>sm</u>oke

<u>sk</u>ull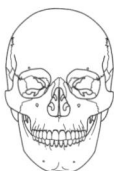

<u>sh</u>ark

<u>sw</u>an

<u>sn</u>ail

<u>ch</u>eese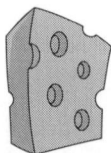

<u>tw</u>ig

<u>cr</u>ow

glove

plate

truck

grapes

spoon

block

pram

screw

scale

brick

spring

church

splash

queen

star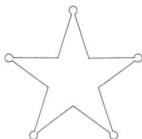

thirteen 13

clown

review

Sound out the first letter of each word. Write the letter in the box.

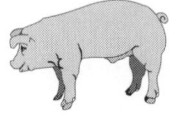

	1		2		3

	4		5		6

	7		8		9

	10		11		12

	13		14		15

	16		17		18

	19		20		21

	22		23		24

Sound out the first <u>two</u> letters of each word. Write both letters in the box.

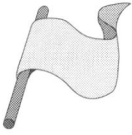 | 1 |

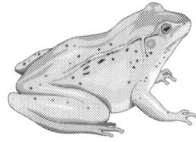 | 2 |

 | 3 |

 | 4 |

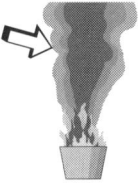 | 5 |

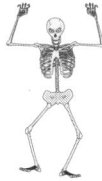 | 6 |

 | 7 |

 | 8 |

 | 9 |

12 | 10 |

 | 11 |

| 12 |

 | 13 |

 | 14 |

 | 15 |

 | 16 |

9

1. [   ]

2. [   ]

3. [   ]

4. [   ]

5. [   ]

6. [   ]

7. [   ]

8. [   ]

9. [   ]

10. [   ]

Sound out the first <u>three</u> letters of each word. Write them in the box.

11. [   ]

12. [   ]

13. [   ]

14. [   ]

15. [   ]

10

Basic List A

Here is a way to learn to spell any new words.

LOOK at the word.

SAY it aloud.

COVER the word.

WRITE it.

CHECK it.

I **am** going home.	**am**
He has **an** apple.	**an**
She is as tall **as** Cathy.	**as**
They are **at** the movies.	**at**
He will **be** there.	**be**
I can **do** the work.	**do**
Do not **go** there.	**go**
He is at work.	**he**
Go **if** you can.	**if**
She **is** a dancer.	**is**
I saw **it**.	**it**
They found **me**.	**me**
This is **my** coat.	**my**
She has **no** food.	**no**
He is fond **of** her.	**of**
They played **on** the field.	**on**
Cathy **or** Mona came along.	**or**
This is **so** heavy.	**so**
He came **to** the hall.	**to**
He ran **up** the hill.	**up**
Help **us**.	**us**

2 Using Sounds

Now let's look at sounds and the simple words that can be formed with them.

Sound out each letter.

be – a – te

| bat |

Sound out each word. Write them in the boxes.

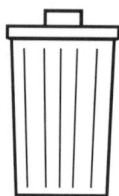

1 | |

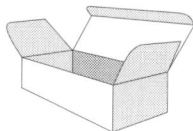

2 | |

3 | |

4 | |

5 | |

6 | |

1 _____

2 _____

3 _____

4 _____

5 _____

6 _____

7 _____

8 _____

9 _____

10 _____

13

1.

2.

3.

4.

5.

6.

7.

8.

9.

10

10.

BUILD A NEW WORD

Sound out the first letter of each word.
Write all three letters in the box to make a new word.

can

1

2

3

4

15

  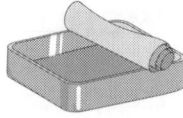

1

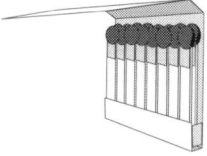  

2

  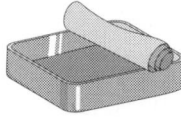

3

4

5

6

16

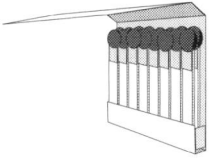  

1

2

3

4

5

6

17

WORD BUILDING

Here, we are changing the first letter to make a new word — a rhyming word.

Write this word   *Use the first sound to make a new word.*

 | **tap** |  | **sap**

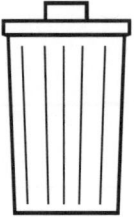 | 1 [ ]

 | 2 [ ]

 | 3 [ ]

 | 4 [ ]

 | 5 [ ]

 | 6 [ ]

 | 7 [ ]

 | 8 [ ]

Here, you change the __second__ letter to make a new word.

Write this word   *Use the first sound to make a new word.*

   bat    i   bit

---

   1 _____

   2 _____

   3 _____

   4 _____

   5 _____

   6 _____

   7 _____

   8 _____

Here, you change the __last__ letter to make a new word.

Write this word **Use the first sound to make a new word.**

tap

tab

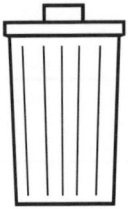
1

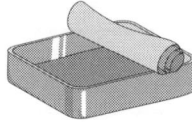
2

3

4

5

6

7

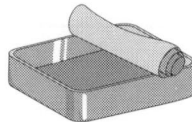
8

20

USING BLENDS

Sound out the whole word.

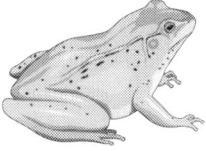 **Let's work out the sounds**
fr – o – ge

frog

1	

2	

3	

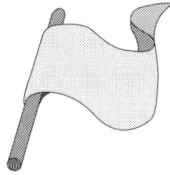

4	

5	

6	

1 _____

12 2 _____

3 _____

4 _____

5 _____

6 _____

7 _____

STOP 8 _____

9 _____

10 _____

Now we are using blends to begin our words.
Sound out the beginning blend or sound of each word. Write all <u>four</u> letters in the box.

slip

sl   —   i   —   p

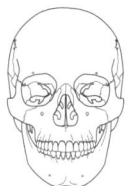  

1.

2.

3.

4.

23

1

2

  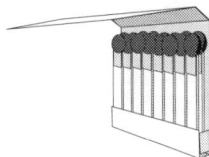

3

4

5

6

24

  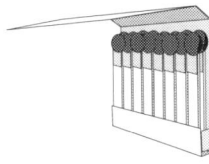

1 _____

  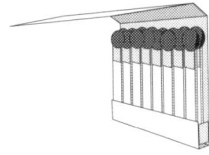

2 _____

3 _____

4 _____

  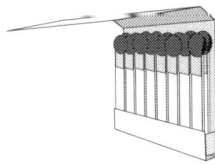

5 _____

  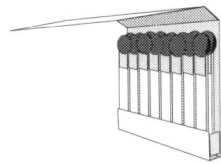

6 _____

Basic List B

**You need to know how to spell these words.
Have someone test you.**

Remember the way
to learn the spelling
of any new word.

LOOK at the word.

SAY it aloud.

COVER the word.

WRITE it.

CHECK it.

all	and	are	ball
been	big	boy	but
can	come	did	dog
doll	down	eat	for
from	get	girl	good
had	has	have	her
here	him	his	home
house	how	know	like
little	look	made	make
man	mother	name	not
now	our	out	over
play	pretty	put	red
run	said	saw	school
see	she	some	take
that	the	them	then
there	they	this	time
too	tree	two	very
was	went	what	when
will	with	would	you

SPELL-CHECK 1

After completing pages 4 to 26, try these short tests.

- *Have someone read each sentence and repeat slowly the word underlined.*

- *Your task is to write each word correctly.*

IA.

They lived in a <u>hut</u>.

The dog hurt its <u>leg</u>.

Take this <u>jar</u> of jam.

The <u>sun</u> shone brightly.

She has a pet <u>cat</u>.

The <u>zip</u> was broken.

The <u>dog</u> is in the yard.

The cat caught the <u>rat</u>.

The <u>van</u> went down the street.

The fish were caught in the <u>net</u>.

IB.

The car will <u>stop</u> here.

They heard the rifle <u>shot</u>.

I saw her <u>trip</u> over.

The plants will <u>grow</u> well.

The tap will <u>drip</u> all night.

Do not <u>slip</u> on the floor.

He will <u>chat</u> to his friend.

I ate the ripe <u>plum</u>.

I heard the timber <u>snap</u>.

They will <u>swim</u> in the creek.

Vowel Sounds

So far we have dealt mainly with short vowel sounds.

> **The short sound of the vowel is usually heard when the word ends in a consonant.**

b<u>a</u>t   l<u>e</u>g   t<u>i</u>n   b<u>o</u>x   g<u>u</u>n

The vowel sounds in these words are short.

> **If a word ends in 'e' the first vowel in the word is usually long and the 'e' is silent.**

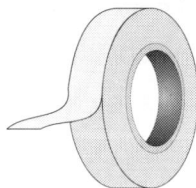

t<u>a</u>p
short vowel

t<u>a</u>pe
long vowel

Here are some other pairs. Say the words aloud. Note the difference in the vowel sounds.

a

mad — made   cap — cape

mat — mate   man — mane

can — cane   fad — fade

e	her — here	pet — pete
i	rid — ride	fin — fine
	bit — bite	pin — pine
	rip — ripe	slim — slime
o	hop — hope	rod — rode
	rob — robe	lob — lobe
	not — note	cop — cope
u	tub — tube	cub — cube
	hug — huge	cut — cute

Here is another rule about vowel sounds.

> **If a word has two vowels together the first is usually long and the second is silent.**

wh<u>ea</u>t

long vowel

c<u>oa</u>ch

long vowel

Here are some other words where the first vowel is long and the second is silent. Say the words aloud. Note the vowel sounds.

ea

deal	east
heal	peach
sneak	bleat
reap	lean

ee

meet	sheep
free	feed
heel	sleeve
fleece	sheen

ai

rain	trail
chain	pain
drain	plain
jail	train

oa

boat	oak
soak	loan
coal	load
cloak	throat

ie

die	tie
lie	tried

Now check this rule.

> The letter pairs '<u>er</u>', '<u>ir</u>', '<u>ur</u>' have the same sound — 'er'.

g<u>ir</u>l   **f<u>er</u>n**   **ch<u>ur</u>ch**

h<u>er</u>d	:	p<u>er</u>ch	:	t<u>er</u>m	:	h<u>er</u>b
tw<u>ir</u>l	:	sh<u>ir</u>t	:	ch<u>ir</u>p	:	f<u>ir</u>m
bl<u>ur</u>	:	c<u>ur</u>b	:	t<u>ur</u>n	:	h<u>ur</u>t

Now look over these:

st<u>ar</u>   **c<u>ar</u>**

The '<u>ar</u>' sound is the same in the following words:

| j<u>ar</u> | : | c<u>ar</u>d | : | d<u>ar</u>k | : | h<u>ar</u>m |
| p<u>ar</u>ty | : | sp<u>ar</u>k | : | y<u>ar</u>n | : | m<u>ar</u>ch |

A. Change each word so that the first vowel in the word is long and the final 'e' is silent.

wag	1 wage	shin	2
slat	3	plan	4
grim	5	hid	6
rid	7	din	8
dot	9	cloth	10

B. Say these words. Is the first vowel long and the second silent? Answer yes or no.

weak	1	crease	2
teeth	3	sheaf	4
waist	5	lain	6
moan	7	foam	8

MORE DOUBLE VOWEL SOUNDS

> The double vowel '**oo**' has two different sounds.

*The long '**oo**' sound.*

 **ball<u>oo</u>n**　　(long sound)

smooth	:	troop	:	boom	:	goose
school	:	food	:	loop	:	soon

*The short '**oo**' sound.*

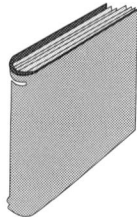 **b<u>oo</u>k**　　(short sound)

wood	:	shook	:	wool	:	look
stood	:	soot	:	hoof	:	hood

> The letter pairs '**<u>oi</u>**' and '**<u>oy</u>**' have the same sound.

 **b<u>oy</u>**　　　 **c<u>oi</u>n**

voice	:	choice	:	toy	:	soil
joy	:	annoy	:	hoist	:	spoil

33

The sounds for '<u>ou</u>' and '<u>ow</u>' can be the same.

 **m<u>ou</u>se**    **c<u>ow</u>**

round	:	count	:	found	:	cloud
sow	:	bow	:	crouch	:	shout
house	:	crowd	:	pouch	:	mound

Another sound for '<u>ow</u>' is the long 'o' sound.

 **b<u>ow</u>**   (long '**o**' sound)

show	:	snow	:	know	:	mower
widow	:	yellow	:	crow	:	window

The sounds for '<u>aw</u>' and '<u>au</u>' are the same.

 **str<u>aw</u>berry**    **s<u>au</u>ce**

claw	:	maul	:	saucer	:	shawl
launch	:	lawn	:	cause	:	hawk

 n**ew**s

 gl**ue**

drew	:	hue	:	crew	:	blue
skewer	:	view	:	fuel	:	dewy

 p**ay**

 th**ey**

prey	:	today	:	stray	:	grey
away	:	obey	:	delay	:	tray

review

1. *Say these words. Do the vowels sound the same as in 'boy' and 'coin'? Write yes or no.*

joint ☐ crunch ☐ moist ☐

scowl ☐ annoy ☐ foil ☐

2. *Say these words. Write them in the column with the matching vowel sound.*

foul, sound, how, below, mellow, cowl, amount, blow, noun, howl

sn<u>ow</u>   **c<u>ow</u>**

_____ | _____
_____ | _____
_____ | _____
_____ | _____
_____ | _____
_____ | _____

3. *Write these words in the column with the matching vowel sound.*

stay, threw, clay, bray, clue review, hay, blue, chew, stray

p<u>ay</u>   **n<u>ew</u>**

_____ | _____
_____ | _____
_____ | _____
_____ | _____

36

Endings

Each group of words has the same ending.
Sound out the last two letters and write them in the box.

hand

band	land
sand	stand
find	bind

1 _____

desk

husk	bask
dusk	tusk
disk	task

2 _____

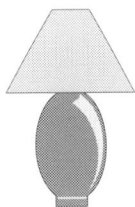

lamp

ramp	limp
camp	stamp
tramp	rump

3 _____

bolt

jolt	kilt
halt	lilt
built	fault

4 _____

fish

dish	hush
wish	trash
wash	cash

5 _____

MORE ENDINGS

Each group of words has the same ending. The ending may consist of two or three letters.

Write the ending in the box.

2 sounds

apple
castle double
table purple
circle bundle

1

stove
save move
five cave
leave give

2

mouse
house spouse
please cheese
loose tease

3

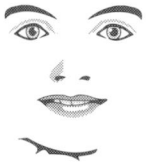
face
place price
twice nice
spice lace

4

stage
cage change
page badge
savage college

5

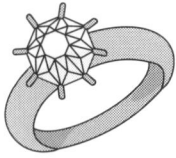 **ring**

sting	fling
bring	cling
spring	ding

 **strong**

song	long
thong	wrong
belong	

 **bang**

hang	sang
fang	slang
clang	tang

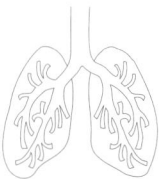 **lung**

sung	flung
bung	stung
slung	hung

 **bunch**

lunch	crunch
punch	drench
bench	stench

 **watch**

catch	latch
match	stretch
stitch	hatch

BUILD A NEW WORD

Use the first two letters of the first picture, a vowel (a, e, i, o, u) and the ending from the second picture.

first 2 letters   vowel   last two letters

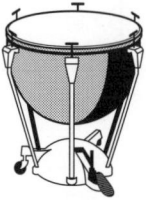

o

or

i

| **drove** |

or

| **drive** |

dr   **ve**

 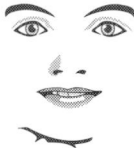

1

2

3

4

1 |

 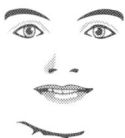

2 |

3 |

 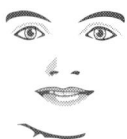

4 |

5 |

6 |

use 3 letter ending

7 |

use 3 letter ending

41

SPELL-CHECK 2

After completing pages 28 to 41 try these short tests:

- *Have someone read each sentence and repeat slowly the word underlined.*

- *Your task – write each word correctly.*

2A.

He <u>can</u> do the work.

The animal was quite <u>tame</u>.

It was a <u>huge</u> building.

The runner was very <u>slim</u>.

They travelled to the <u>east</u>.

I will <u>feed</u> the cats.

The <u>rain</u> poured down.

The sky was very <u>dark</u>.

I saw the <u>girl</u>.

The car will <u>turn</u> the corner.

She ate the <u>food</u>.

The <u>soil</u> is very poor here.

The <u>cloud</u> is very large.

I saw the <u>hawk</u> in the sky.

The <u>tray</u> was empty.

2B.

He hurt his <u>hand</u>.

It was a <u>silk</u> cloth.

The <u>lamp</u> was lit at night.

The ground was very <u>soft</u>.

He bought her a <u>gift</u>.

I <u>think</u> he will go.

They played <u>chess</u>.

They did not <u>trust</u> him.

She played a <u>trick</u> on her friend.

He threw the <u>stick</u>.

The boat will <u>drift</u> out to sea.

The <u>cave</u> was very dark.

They walked onto the <u>stage</u>.

He was <u>stung</u> by a bee.

The work was done <u>twice</u>.

Rhyming Words

In this section, you are going to create families of rhyming words.

Here's an example:

cat

| b**at** | f**at** | m**at** |
| r**at** | s**at** | p**at** |

sack

1.

| b_____ | p_____ | r_____ |
| l_____ | t_____ | st_____ |

man

2.

| r_____ | c_____ | th_____ |
| sc_____ | pl_____ | sp_____ |

bell

3.

| w_____ | s_____ | t_____ |
| sh_____ | sp_____ | sm_____ |

ball

4.

| t_____ | c_____ | f_____ |
| h_____ | st_____ | sm_____ |

43

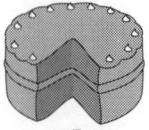
cake

1. | l _____ | t _____ | m _____ |
   | sn _____ | sh _____ | dr _____ |

shark

2. | b _____ | m _____ | p _____ |
   | d _____ | sp _____ | st _____ |

gate

3. | l _____ | h _____ | m _____ |
   | sk _____ | pl _____ | cr _____ |

10
ten

4. | m _____ | p _____ | d _____ |
   | wh _____ | th _____ | h _____ |

play

5. | d _____ | m _____ | s _____ |
   | tr _____ | st _____ | spr _____ |

sit

6. | h _____ | b _____ | f _____ |
   | sp _____ | fl _____ | sl _____ |

pet

7. | g _____ | m _____ | w _____ |
   | n _____ | b _____ | fr _____ |

44

pill

1.

w	f	k
dr	fr	gr

spot

2.

n	g	l
sh	pl	sl

bun

3.

f	r	g
sp	st	sh

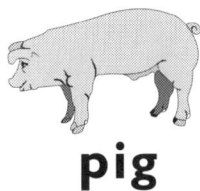

pig

4.

d	r	f
j	spr	tw

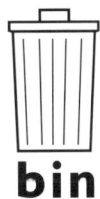

bin

5.

w	f	t
th	sp	sh

dog

6.

l	j	h
f	sl	cl

bow

7.

l	m	gr
sh	sl	fl

45

flame

1.

| s _____ | g _____ | t _____ |
| c _____ | n _____ | sh _____ |

shade

2.

| m _____ | f _____ | j _____ |
| tr _____ | bl _____ | sp _____ |

bike

3.

| h _____ | l _____ | p _____ |
| str _____ | sp _____ | tr _____ |

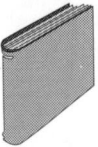

book

4.

| l _____ | t _____ | c _____ |
| sh _____ | cr _____ | br _____ |

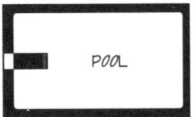

POOL

pool

5.

| t _____ | c _____ | f _____ |
| st _____ | sch _____ | sp _____ |

boat

6.

| c _____ | g _____ | m _____ |
| fl _____ | gl _____ | thr _____ |

sheep

7.

| d _____ | p _____ | w _____ |
| sl _____ | st _____ | sw _____ |

46

gown

1	d ____	t ____	br ____
	fr ____	cr ____	dr ____

band

2	l ____	h ____	st ____
	gr ____	br ____	str ____

flew

3	f ____	n ____	cr ____
	br ____	bl ____	st ____

light

4	f ____	t ____	m ____
	sl ____	fl ____	fr ____

pick

5	l ____	s ____	ch ____
	tr ____	sl ____	th ____

stump

6	l ____	b ____	s ____
	th ____	cl ____	sl ____

bride

7	h ____	s ____	t ____
	r ____	sl ____	str ____

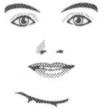

face

1.
p	l	r
gr	sp	pl

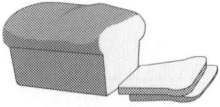

crust

2.
j	m	r
d	tr	thr

lunch

3.
p	m	b
h	br	cr

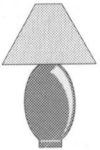

lamp

4.
d	r	c
st	cr	ch

bed

5.
f	l	r
sl	fl	bl

cod

6.
n	s	p
r	sh	pl

bag

7.
r	t	l
w	st	cr

For each word given, write as many rhyming words as you can.

ball

1
_____
_____

10
ten

2
_____
_____

dog

3
_____
_____

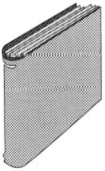

book

4
_____
_____

stump

5
_____
_____

MORE RHYMING WORDS

bug

1.   t _____   r _____   h _____
     sn _____   pl _____   sl _____

hut

2.   n _____   c _____   b _____
     j _____   sh _____   str _____

ham

3.   r _____   d _____   j _____
     cr _____   gr _____   tr _____

him

4.   r _____   d _____   br _____
     gr _____   tr _____   sl _____

drum

5.   h _____   r _____   g _____
     pl _____   gl _____   sc _____

cap

6.   m _____   n _____   s _____
     tr _____   sl _____   str _____

zip

7.   n _____   h _____   t _____
     sh _____   sl _____   str _____

50

stop

1. h _____   m _____   t _____
   sl _____   sh _____   ch _____

crab

2. j _____   t _____   c _____
   dr _____   st _____   sc _____

cob

3. s _____   r _____   j _____
   bl _____   sl _____   thr _____

tub

4. r _____   h _____   c _____
   gr _____   sn _____   shr _____

neck

5. d _____   p _____   ch _____
   fl _____   sp _____   wr _____

lock

6. d _____   r _____   s _____
   st _____   bl _____   ch _____

duck

7. l _____   m _____   s _____
   tr _____   st _____   str _____

MORE RHYMING

Complete these rhyming words.
Don't forget to say the words aloud.

spend

1
| b _____ | m _____ | l _____ |
| f _____ | tr _____ | bl _____ |

tent

2
| l _____ | b _____ | r _____ |
| w _____ | d _____ | sp _____ |

punt

3
| h _____ | r _____ | st _____ |
| sh _____ | bl _____ | br _____ |

nest

4
| r _____ | p _____ | t _____ |
| b _____ | ch _____ | cr _____ |

mint

5
| h _____ | t _____ | l _____ |
| gl _____ | fl _____ | pr _____ |

trunk

6
| h _____ | j _____ | s _____ |
| cl _____ | b _____ | shr _____ |

bang

1. g_____ s_____ h_____
   sl_____ cl_____ spr_____

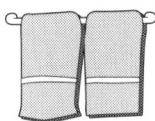
hung

2. l_____ r_____ s_____
   st_____ fl_____ str_____

brush

3. h_____ l_____ r_____
   cr_____ fl_____ pl_____

tank

4. b_____ r_____ s_____
   sp_____ pl_____ shr_____

cash

5. d_____ l_____ s_____
   cr_____ cl_____ sm_____

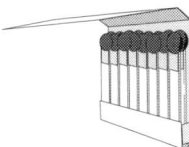
match

6. c_____ b_____ l_____
   h_____ sn_____ scr_____

witch

7. d_____ p_____ h_____
   sw_____ tw_____ st_____

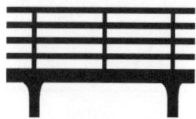

seat

1. | h _____ | m _____ | tr _____ |
   | wh _____ | pl _____ | bl _____ |

queen

2. | s _____ | k _____ | b _____ |
   | sh _____ | scr _____ | gr _____ |

beam

3. | r _____ | t _____ | cr _____ |
   | st _____ | dr _____ | scr _____ |

rain

4. | g _____ | p _____ | l _____ |
   | pl _____ | br _____ | str _____ |

broom

5. | r _____ | b _____ | l _____ |
   | d _____ | gl _____ | gr _____ |

nail

6. | b _____ | p _____ | r _____ |
   | fr _____ | tr _____ | sn _____ |

moon

7. | n _____ | s _____ | b _____ |
   | cr _____ | sp _____ | sw _____ |

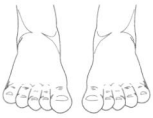
feet

1.
m	sl	gr
sw	fl	str

oil

2.
t	b	c
f	sp	br

saw

3.
r	p	l
dr	str	cl

leek

4.
p	r	w
m	ch	sl

trout

5.
b	r	sp
st	sc	cl

steed

6.
n	r	h
s	bl	gr

peak

7.
w	b	l
sp	bl	str

55

review

For each word given, write as many rhyming words as you can.

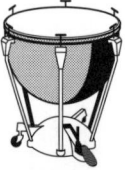

drum

1 _____

_____

stop

2 _____

_____

nest

3 _____

_____

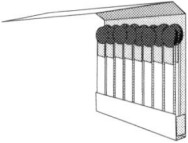

match

4 _____

_____

tub

5 _____

_____

review

Write each word using the sound and letter clues. Under the word you have written write a rhyming word.

Here is a sample.

initial sounds (2)	vowel sound	ending
		**nt**

spent
went

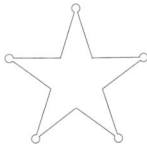  **nk**

1.

  **nd**

2.

  **sh**

3.

  **ng**

4.

  **nk**

5.

57

  **nd** 1.

  **ng** 2.

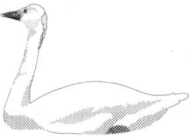  **tch** 3.

  **ce** 4.

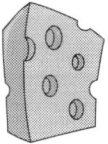  **nk** 5.

  **sh** 6.

  **ft** 7.

58

BUILDING WITH BLENDS

The last section of rhyming words.

Once again, don't forget to say the words aloud.

1	**joke**	br ___	sp ___	str ___
2	**gale**	st ___	wh ___	sc ___
3	**long**	th ___	pr ___	str ___
4	**cart**	d ___	ch ___	st ___
5	**cove**	st ___	gr ___	dr ___
6	**care**	sp ___	st ___	sc ___
7	**face**	gr ___	sp ___	tr ___
8	**hope**	sl ___	gr ___	sc ___
9	**like**	h ___	str ___	sp ___

1	**cute**	l _____	fl _____	br _____
2	**jeer**	ch _____	st _____	sn _____
3	**boot**	l _____	sh _____	sc _____
4	**find**	b _____	gr _____	bl _____
5	**ape**	gr _____	sh _____	scr _____
6	**air**	ch _____	fl _____	st _____
7	**fear**	cl _____	sh _____	sp _____
8	**dine**	tw _____	sp _____	wh _____
9	**able**	f _____	g _____	st _____
10	**dive**	dr _____	str _____	thr _____
11	**pipe**	sw _____	tr _____	str _____

1 **sane**	c ___	w ___	l ___
2 **hoop**	sn ___	tr ___	st ___
3 **time**	cr ___	gr ___	pr ___
4 **bone**	st ___	dr ___	pr ___
5 **cave**	sl ___	gr ___	sh ___
6 **rose**	th ___	ch ___	pr ___
7 **file**	sm ___	wh ___	m ___
8 **toss**	m ___	fl ___	gl ___
9 **mark**	sp ___	sh ___	st ___
10 **took**	sh ___	cr ___	br ___
11 **bought**	s ___	br ___	th ___

review

Write each word using the sound and letter clues. Under the word you have written write two rhyming words.

Here is a sample.

initial sounds (2)   vowel sounds   ending

  **ne**

spine
line
mine

1.

  **me**

2.

  **le**

3.

  **rk**

4.

  **nd**

5.

  **ve**

62

initial sounds (2)	vowel sounds	ending	
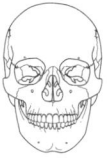		**rt**	1
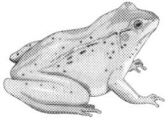		**me**	2
		**te**	3
		**nk**	4
		**ng**	5
		**tch**	6
		**ft**	7

63

Basic List C

You need to know how to spell these words.
Have someone test you.

Use the

- **LOOK**
- **SAY**
- **COVER**
- **WRITE**
- **CHECK**

method.

about	after	again	air
another	around	asked	away
back	before	because	came
children	could	called	car
day	does	door	each
every	end	find	first
friend	father	found	going
gave	help	heard	happy
into	inside	just	long
live	last	left	later
lunch	many	more	most
morning	much	must	night
next	new	nice	never
off	old	one	only
other	once	people	place
put	picture	ran	right
small	sleep	same	say
sound	soon	tell	their
these	through	thought	things
took	told	think	than
use	until	water	way
well	were	where	which
who	why	work	write
while	yes		

SPELL-CHECK 3

3A.

They walked along the <u>track</u>.

They had a <u>plan</u>.

He will <u>shake</u> the rattle.

<u>When</u> will she go?

He had a <u>crate</u> of books.

She <u>spun</u> the wheel.

The <u>frog</u> is in the garden.

The huge truck was very <u>slow</u>.

He <u>shook</u> the bag.

It was a <u>steep</u> hill.

There is the <u>brown</u> house.

The <u>smoke</u> came from the pipe.

The <u>clock</u> was on the wall.

There is a <u>thick</u> piece of timber.

The cow will <u>plod</u> along the track.

SPELL-CHECK 3

3B.

The pencil was <u>blunt</u>.

Jona will <u>crush</u> the box.

Jim will <u>switch</u> on the light.

She had a strange <u>dream</u>.

They followed the <u>trail</u>.

Can you <u>draw</u> the picture?

It was a <u>bleak</u> day.

They will <u>start</u> the car.

The <u>stove</u> is new.

The <u>spear</u> had a sharp point.

I will <u>stoop</u> down and pick it up.

There was a <u>shark</u> in the water.

She played the <u>flute</u>.

The boat will <u>drift</u> away.

She bought a new <u>skirt</u>.

Silent Letters

Say each word. Circle the silent letter.

1

 knife

 knee

 knight

 knot

---

2

 comb

 lamb

 thumb

 limb

67

 yolk

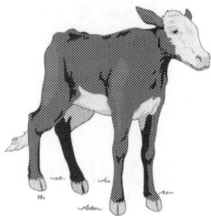 calf

 half

 palm

 gnome

 sign

 gnu

 gnat

1

 ghost

 heir

 hour

 vehicle

---

2

 scissors

 muscle

 scent

 scene

---

3

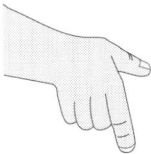 wrist

 sword

2 two

 wrap

69

Blends & Endings

1. Sound out the initial blend.

2. Join the blend to these stems.

3. Write each new word.

ap	ip	**slap**	**slip**
op	ot	**slop**	**slot**
ow	ave	**slow**	**slave**
	eeve		**sleeve**

1.

ag	oat	_____	_____
oor	our	_____	_____
ake	ick	_____	_____
	ash		_____

2.

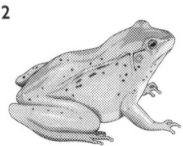

om	ont	_____	_____
ost	ee	_____	_____
ill	uit	_____	_____
	own		_____

3.

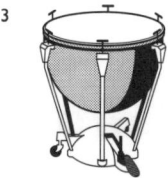

op	aw	_____	_____
ug	ain	_____	_____
eam	ive	_____	_____
	ess		_____

4.

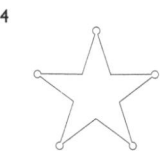

ain	ate	_____	_____
arch	ill	_____	_____
art	one	_____	_____
	ory		_____

1   ace eed   _____ _____
       oon ort   _____ _____
       ark end   _____ _____
         oke   _____

2   ock ack   _____ _____
       ind ade   _____ _____
       ood ast   _____ _____
         ank   _____

3   obe ide   _____ _____
       int owl   _____ _____
       ime ize   _____ _____
         ice   _____

4   at en   _____ _____
       ile elk   _____ _____
       ite ale   _____ _____
         eat   _____

5   ar are   _____ _____
       ale arf   _____ _____
       ore oop   _____ _____
         out   _____

6   at op   _____ _____
       ill eck   _____ _____
       air ild   _____ _____
         art   _____

1
iet   ite
ick   ack
ake   ilt
est
_____ _____
_____ _____
_____ _____
_____

2
op   amp
oss   own
owd   ash
ater
_____ _____
_____ _____
_____ _____
_____

3
ade   ad
ean   ass
obe   eam
ance
_____ _____
_____ _____
_____ _____
_____

4
ace   ane
ant   ush
ank   ead
astic
_____ _____
_____ _____
_____ _____
_____

5
uce   ade
ain   ibe
ied   ust
ash
_____ _____
_____ _____
_____ _____
_____

6
een   eat
ant   oup
ound   ain
asp
_____ _____
_____ _____
_____ _____
_____

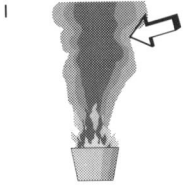

1.
all   art
ash   ell
ile   ack
       ooth
_____ _____
_____ _____
_____ _____
       _____

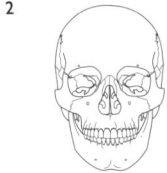

2.
ip   in
unk   ill
irt   ate
       etch
_____ _____
_____ _____
_____ _____
       _____

3.
ell   oes
iny   ave
ore   oot
       ape
_____ _____
_____ _____
_____ _____
       _____

4.
im   ay
eet   eep
ift   ipe
       amp
_____ _____
_____ _____
_____ _____
       _____

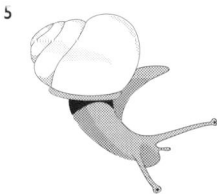

5.
ap   ag
ack   arl
ake   eak
       atch
_____ _____
_____ _____
_____ _____
       _____

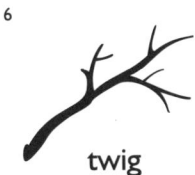

6.
in   ice
ist   eak
eet   eed
       itch

twig
_____ _____
_____ _____
_____ _____
       _____

73

1

ead	eak	_____	_____
ing	oke	_____	_____
oom	own	_____	_____
eeze		_____	

2

ay	ip	_____	_____
ock	ass	_____	_____
ose	imb	_____	_____
othes		_____	

Use the first three sounds for these.

3

ing	ain	**spring**	_____
ay	ead	_____	_____
int	inkle	_____	_____

4

eam	um	**scream**	_____
rub	ape	_____	_____
atch	aps	_____	_____

5

at	ash	**splat**	_____
ice	int	_____	_____
it	otch	_____	_____

6

ong	eet	**strong**	_____
and	ing	_____	_____
eam	oke	_____	_____

74

review

Look at the picture. Write the initial blend. Use the stems to form two words. Only two of the stems will make 'real' words.

Here is an example.

initial blend	stem	two correct words
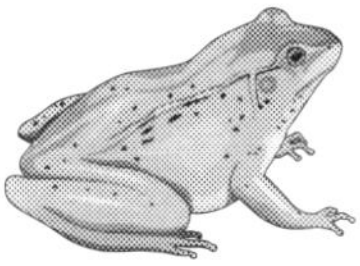 **fr**	own ive ess uit eam	**frown** **fruit**

	our eeve om art ate	1

	obe oke ime end ale	2

	ark ile eat ve ab	3

	eck obe ize ild een	4

75

ade	ash	1
ant	owd	
atch		

ass	ust	2
een	owd	
ash		

ick	oup	3
asp	ilt	
ag		

iny	ice	4
oke	oot	
arl		

ist	arl	5
eed	eet	
atch		

oke	ift	6
in	oes	
eeze		

in	ock	7
all	ass	
irt		

76

Singular & Plural

The word 'singular' means <u>one</u>.
The word 'plural' means <u>more than one</u>.

> **Most words change from the singular to the plural by adding 's'.**

Add '<u>s</u>':

cat
(singular)

cat<u>s</u>
(plural)

> **For words ending in 's', 'sh', 'ch', 'x', or 'z, add '<u>es</u>'.**

Add '<u>es</u>':

bus — bus<u>es</u>

torch — torch<u>es</u>

smash — smash<u>es</u>

fox — fox<u>es</u>

77

> For words ending in 'y' which have a consonant before the 'y', change 'y' to 'i' before adding '**es**'.

*Change 'y' to 'i' before adding '**es**':*

fly — fl**ies**

pony — pon**ies**

baby — babies

> For words ending in 'y' with the vowel 'a', 'e', or 'o' in front of the 'y', the 'y' does <u>not</u> change.

*Add '**s**' to words ending in 'y':*

toy — toy**s**

tray — tray**s**

donkey — donkey**s**

> For words which end in 'f' or 'fe', the 'f' changes to 'v' and 'es' is added.

*Add '**es**' to words ending in 'f':*

$$\frac{1}{2}$$

half — hal**ves**

knife — kni**ves**

scarf — scar**ves**

> For words ending in 'o', some of them simply add '**s**' while others add '**es**'.

*Add '**s**' to words ending in 'o':*

piano — pianos

photo — photos

banjo — banjos

*Add '**es**' to words ending in 'o':*

dingo — dingoes

tomato – tomatoes

volcano — volcanoes

The most common words ending in 'o' are listed below:

zero	— zeroes	cargo	— cargoes
solo	— solos	mango	— mangoes
merino	— merinos	potato	— potatoes
silo	— silos	tomato	— tomatoes

> For words made up of two or three parts, 's' is usually added to the first part.

*Add '**s**' to compound words:*

mother-in-law — mothers-in-law

daughter-in-law — daughters-in-law

Irregular plurals:

man — men

woman — women

foot — feet

mouse — mice

tooth — teeth

goose — geese

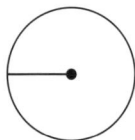

ox — oxen

child — children

cactus — cacti

radius — radii

octopus — octopii

No change words:

sheep — sheep

innings — innings

deer — deer

salmon — salmon

trousers — trousers

fish — fish

scissors — scissors

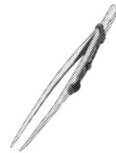

tweezers — tweezers

81

review

A. Write the plural form of these words.

cross   1 [ ]   tax   2 [ ]

girl   3 [ ]   daisy   4 [ ]

circus   5 [ ]   loaf   6 [ ]

lion   7 [ ]   launch   8 [ ]

beach   9 [ ]   life   10 [ ]

lolly   11 [ ]   photo   12 [ ]

wish   13 [ ]   bus   14 [ ]

whale   15 [ ]   thief   16 [ ]

sheep   17 [ ]   journey   18 [ ]

jersey   19 [ ]   echo   20 [ ]

B. _____

factory   1 [ ]   injury   2 [ ]

lady   3 [ ]   berry   4 [ ]

valley   5 [ ]   jockey   6 [ ]

relay   7 [ ]   gully   8 [ ]

memory   9 [ ]   buoy   10 [ ]

army   11 [ ]   city   12 [ ]

Word Endings

Three of the most common endings are s, ed and ing.

These words are verbs.

base word	plural	past	present
	s	ed	ing
water	waters	watered	watering
cook	cooks	cooked	cooking
play	plays	played	playing
seat	seats	seated	seating

Words ending in 'e', just add 'd' for past and 'e' is dropped for present.

hope	hopes	hoped	hoping
taste	tastes	tasted	tasting
use	uses	used	using

Words that have double letters (they often end in 'n' or 'p').

tap	taps	tapped	tapping
flap	flaps	flapped	flapping
plan	plans	planned	planning

Words ending in 'y'.

spy	spies	spied	spying
study	studies	studied	studying
dry	dries	dried	drying

review

A. Use the correct form of the word in brackets to complete each sentence.

Here is an example.

The girl was (kick) __**kicking**__ the ball.

1. Has the food been (cook) _____ yet?

2. The child was (trick) _____ into going the wrong way.

3. After (enter) _____ the room all the guests sat down.

4. She (smile) _____ happily at her favourite pets.

5. They had (plan) _____ the trip for many months.

6. The boys were (rip) _____ up all the old papers.

7. The burglar had (spy) _____ on the house for days.

8. The potter (shape) _____ the clay carefully.

9. They were (hope) _____ to be home by six o'clock.

10. She was not (worry) _____ by the loss of the money.

review

B. Complete this table.

base word	plural s	past ed	present ing
1 howl			
2 joke			
3 drip			
4 reply			
5 smile			
6 place			
7 rest			
8 enter			
9 walk			
10 load			
11 rip			
12 dry			

SPELL-CHECK 4

After completing pages 67 to 85 try these short tests.

- *Have someone read each sentence and repeat slowly the word underlined.*
- *Your task — write each word correctly.*

4A. He hurt his <u>knee</u>.
The <u>lamb</u> was in the paddock.
She took <u>half</u> the food away.
It was a large <u>sign</u>.
The boys climbed the <u>palm</u> tree.
She bought the garden <u>gnome</u>.
They admired the beautiful <u>scene</u>.
Can you <u>wrap</u> the parcel?
She read the <u>story</u>.
They bought a box of <u>fruit</u>.
The water flowed down the <u>drain</u>.
She will <u>check</u> the work.
The <u>crown</u> was in the case.
She <u>tried</u> to do the work.
He will <u>twist</u> the piece of steel.

4B. They <u>loaded</u> the truck.
The work was <u>planned</u> well.
The girl <u>studied</u> the work.
After <u>entering</u> the room she sat down.
The water <u>dripped</u> onto the floor.
They were <u>hoping</u> to finish the work.
She <u>spied</u> the boat in the harbour.
The <u>foxes</u> ran into the forest.
Are the <u>torches</u> on the shelf.
They rode the <u>ponies</u> in the show.
Is the <u>donkey</u> in the yard?
The <u>knives</u> were sharp.
All the group climbed the <u>cliffs</u>.
They fed the <u>geese</u>.
I saw the <u>deer</u> at the zoo.

PREFIXES

A prefix is a syllable at the beginning of a word.

'**mis**' is a prefix which means wrong or incorrect.

misspell   means *to spell incorrectly.*

Here are some common prefixes and their meanings:

prefix	meaning	sample word
en	to make	**encircle** (to make a circle around)
mid	the middle of	**midday** (the middle of the day)
un	not or the opposite of	**untidy** (not tidy)
over	above or beyond	**overcharge** (to charge above the correct price)
under	beneath	**underground** (beneath the ground)
fore	before	**forewarn** (to warn before)
out	beyond	**outrun** (to run beyond another or faster than another)
up	upwards	**upturn** (to turn upwards)

prefix	meaning	sample word
re	back or again	**repay** (to pay back)
in	not	**incurable** (not able to be cured)
inter	between	**intercept** (to take between)
sub	under	**submerge** (to go under water)
pro	further forward	**progress** (to go forward)
ex	out of	**export** (to send out of a country)
con	with or together	**connect** (to join together)
pre	before	**precede** (to go before)
de	down, further away	**descend** (to go down)

Underline the prefix.

enrich	midnight	uphill	reduce
exclaim	underneath	conduct	overpay
project	unclean	outlay	insane
prefer	decay	subway	forecast

SUFFIXES

A suffix is a syllable at the end of a word.

'**or**' is a suffix which means <u>one who</u>.

sailor   means *one who sails*

Here are some common suffixes and their meanings:

sufix	meaning	sample word
er	one who	**builder** (one who builds)
or	one who	**actor** (one who acts)
en	made of	**woollen** (made of wool)
ful	full of	**hopeful** (full of hope)
en	to make	**deepen** (to make deep)
fy	to make	**purify** (to make pure)
ant	one who	**assistant** (one who assists)
ist	one who	**florist** (one who sells flowers)
less	without	**fearless** (without fear)
se	to make	**cleanse** (to make clean)
hood	state of being	**childhood** (state of being a child)

sufix	meaning	sample word
ment	state of being	**contentment** (state of being happy)
th	state of being	**length** (state of being long)
ish	rather or like	**foolish** (like a fool)
ous	full of	**dangerous** (full of danger)
ion	the act of	**extension** (the act of making larger)
able	capable	**portable** (capable of being carried)
al	belonging to	**annual** (belonging to a year)
ee	one who is	**employee** (one who is employed)
en	made of	**golden** (made of gold)

Underline the suffix.

hopeless	painter	strength	careful
brotherhood	drinkable	polish	refugee
wooden	simplify	silken	actor
enjoyment	perilous	artist	lengthen
legal	action	management	baker

USING SYLLABLES

When spelling long words, it can be useful to break the word into syllables.

There are three easy rules to follow when breaking words into syllables.

> **1. When there are double consonants.**

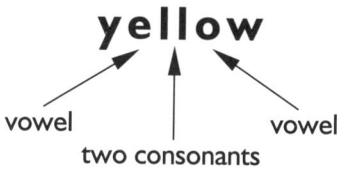

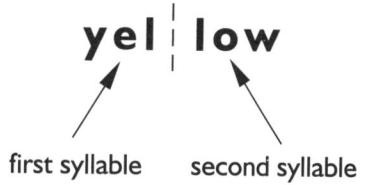

yellow

vowel — two consonants — vowel

yel | low

first syllable — second syllable

Here are some examples:

bal | loon   sum | mer   rib | bon   wel | come

blan | ket   har | vest   am | bush   can | teen

Mark the syllables in these words:

1 skipper	common	traffic	hidden
2 petrol	cactus	island	picnic
3 signal	tractor	bullet	button
4 whisper	berry	written	thunder
5 company	fragment	escape	cottage
6 buffalo	matter	tunnel	anvil
7 artistic	circumvent		

91

2. When there is one consonant between two vowels.

motel

vowel — consonant — vowel

mo|tel

first syllable   second syllable

Here are some examples:

mu | sic	pi | lot	ba | sic	ba | bies
re | fer	du | ties	ra | tion	ba | sin

Mark the syllables in these words:

1 nation   clover   ocean   ladies
2 piper   pirate   native   stoker
3 lunar   region   female   agent
4 cubic   local   erase   ruler

3. When a word ends in 'le'.

needle

consonant   ending 'le'

nee|dle

first syllable   second syllable

Here are some examples:

hus | tle	sad | dle	han | dle	sim | ple
can | dle	cas | tle	cat | tle	an | kle
a | ble	jun | gle	jin | gle	whis | tle

review

A. Mark the syllables in these words:

1 princess	exclaim	ailment	fabric
2 important	winter	berries	captive
3 frequent	domain	rattle	cradle
4 ocean	nation	vibrate	jasmine

B. Are the syllables in these words marked correctly:

1 stu ¦ pid	vi ¦ tal	bl ¦ ister	rib ¦ bon
2 ma ¦ chine	lol ¦ ly	sev ¦ en	not ¦ ice
3 set ¦ tle	scra ¦ mble	pros ¦ per	bu ¦ sy
4 se ¦ cond	bu ¦ tton	curr ¦ ent	ob ¦ ject

C. Break the word into syllables and write the word.

1

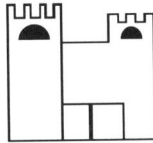
2

3

4

D. Now break these longer words into syllables.

1 incredible	professor	important	fantastic
2 hospitality	studying	uneasiness	contentment
3 unoccupied	exception	singular	contractions

93

COMPOUND WORDS

> Compound words are made from two or more words.

Check these examples.

cow + girl

| **cowgirl** |

light + house

| **lighthouse** |

sun + flower

| **sunflower** |

foot + ball

| **football** |

Compound words formed with 'some':

		one		someone
some	+	thing	⇨	something
		body		somebody
		time		sometime

Compound words formed with 'every':

		one		everyone
every	+	thing	⇨	everything
		body		everybody
		time		everytime

Compound words formed with 'any':

		one		anyone
any	+	thing	⇨	anything
		body		anybody
		time		anytime

Write compound words using the pictures as a key.

1.

2.

3.

4.

5.

6.

7.

8.

9.

10.

95

review

A. Match a word in the circle to a word in the box to make a compound word.

1.
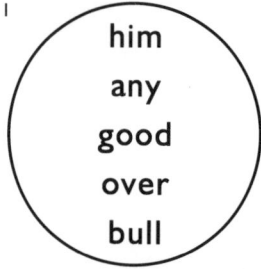 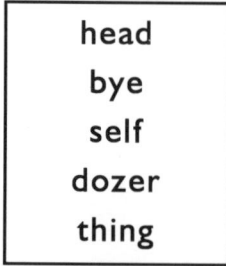

him	head
any	bye
good	self
over	dozer
bull	thing

_____

_____

_____

_____

_____

2.

jack	apple
pine	side
my	knife
sea	self
home	wards

_____

_____

_____

_____

_____

3.
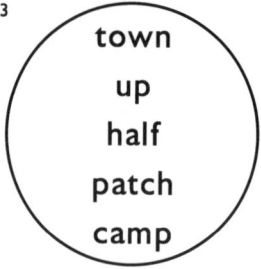 

town	work
up	way
half	ship
patch	stairs
camp	fire

_____

_____

_____

_____

_____

B. Write two compound words using the picture as a key.

1. [   ]

2. [   ]

C. Add a second word to create compound words.

head _____   rain _____   bed _____

96

Basic List D

This list contains some tricky words that often cause trouble. Study the list and then have someone test you.

Remember the

- LOOK
- SAY
- COVER
- WRITE
- CHECK

method.

ache	again	always	among
answer	any	been	beginning
believe	blue	break	built
business	busy	buy	can't
choose	colour	coming	cough
could	country	dear	doctor
does	done	don't	early
easy	enough	every	February
forty	friend	guess	half
having	hear	heard	here
hoarse	hour	instead	just
knew	know	laid	loose
lose	making	many	meant
minute	much	none	often
once	piece	raise	read
ready	said	says	seems
separate	shoes	since	some
straight	sugar	sure	tear
their	there	they	though
through	tired	tonight	too
trouble	truly	Tuesday	two
used	very	wear	Wednesday
week	where	whether	which
whole	women	won't	would
write	writing	wrote	

SPELL-CHECK 5

After completing pages 83 to 97 try these two short tests.

- *Have someone read each sentence and repeat slowly the word underlined.*

- *Your task – write each word correctly.*

5A. It is now <u>midday</u>.
He will <u>outrun</u> his brother.
Please <u>return</u> the book.
They will <u>import</u> a new car.
They travelled on the <u>subway</u>.
There was a <u>protest</u> march.
He will <u>demand</u> payment.
They ran <u>uphill</u>.
She is a fine <u>sailor</u>.
It was a <u>wooden</u> cabinet.
She became a famous <u>artist</u>.
The <u>silken</u> scarf was very beautiful.
The movie was full of <u>action</u>.
It was a <u>remarkable</u> story.
She had exciting <u>childhood</u> experiences.

5B. The book is <u>hidden</u> under the desk.
It is a <u>proper</u> coin.
They will <u>punish</u> the criminal.
There is a strong <u>current</u> in the creek.
They had <u>dinner</u> early.
She will <u>protect</u> the small kitten.
He was <u>absent</u> from school yesterday.
The <u>rocket</u> was fired into the air.
There is the <u>capital</u> city.
His work was greatly <u>improved</u>.
It is <u>impossible</u> to complete the work.
She is <u>visiting</u> her niece.
They had a <u>wonderful</u> time.
She went <u>upstairs</u>.
They set off <u>homewards</u>.
The <u>newspaper</u> has been delivered.

> Words which have letter/s left out with an apostrophe are called contractions.

she will — she'll

letters left out – <u>wi</u>

Contractions involving <u>has</u>, <u>had</u> and <u>have</u>.

(has)	he's	she's
(had)	I'd	he'd she'd you'd we'd they'd
(have)	I've	you've we've they've

Contractions involving <u>not</u>.

haven't   hasn't   can't   aren't   needn't   mustn't   mightn't   shouldn't   couldn't   wouldn't   doesn't   don't   isn't

Contractions involving <u>will</u> or <u>shall</u>.

I'll   he'll   she'll   we'll   they'll

Contractions involving <u>is</u> or <u>are</u>.

(is)	he's	she's	it's	that's	there's
(are)	you're	we're	they're		

Write the shortened form of the words underlined.

1   I know <u>she is</u> waiting at the gate.

2   <u>We had</u> finished the work.

3   <u>They have</u> gone home.

4   <u>She will</u> go to the movies.

5   <u>That is</u> the correct answer.

6   <u>You are</u> going home.

Frequently Misspelt Words

Ending <u>aught</u>:

He <u>caught</u> the ball.	**caught**
She <u>taught</u> him the piano.	**taught**
My <u>daughter</u> visited her.	**daughter**
Spot is a <u>naughty</u> dog.	**naughty**

Ending <u>ought</u>:

She <u>bought</u> the present.	**bought**
They <u>fought</u> in the ring.	**fought**
I <u>thought</u> I saw him.	**thought**
She <u>brought</u> the parcel with her.	**brought**

<u>there</u>, <u>their</u>:

I saw <u>their</u> house.	**their**
Did you take <u>their</u> books?	**their**
<u>Their</u> pencils are on the desk.	**their**
She is <u>there</u>.	**there**
<u>There</u> are the books.	**there**
Was <u>there</u> anyone in the house?	**there**
Were <u>there</u> any children at the shop?	**there**

<u>though</u>, <u>through</u>, <u>thought</u>:

<u>Though</u> he was sick he finished the work.	**though**
I went <u>though</u> I didn't want to.	**though**
She walked <u>through</u> the bush.	**through**
The ball went <u>through</u> the window.	**through**
She <u>thought</u> she had the answer.	**thought**
Have you <u>thought</u> out the problem?	**thought**

receipt *and* receive:

Here is the <u>receipt</u> for the petrol.	**receipt**
Did you collect the <u>receipt</u>?	**receipt**
The girl will <u>receive</u> the prize.	**receive**
Has she been able to <u>receive</u> the present?	**receive**

practice *and* practise:

She will <u>practise</u> the piano.	**practise**
<u>Practise</u> the dance now.	**practise**
He always did plenty of <u>practice</u>.	**practice**
The <u>practice</u> took two hours.	**practice**

chose *and* choose:

He <u>chose</u> a new suit.	**chose**
I <u>chose</u> it last week.	**chose**
Could you <u>choose</u> a new book?	**choose**
Sue will <u>choose</u> a new dress.	**choose**

bought *and* brought:

They <u>bought</u> the new car last week.	**bought**
Has she <u>bought</u> any vegetables?	**bought**
The boy <u>brought</u> the parcel home.	**brought**
Has the clock been <u>brought</u> back to the house?	**brought**

past *and* passed:

Many of them walked <u>past</u> the shop.	**past**
The car travelled <u>past</u> the intersection.	**past**
The sportscar <u>passed</u> the line of traffic.	**passed**
Has your brother <u>passed</u> his driving test?	**passed**

lose *and* loose:

She will <u>lose</u> the race.	**lose**
Did the boy <u>lose</u> any money?	**lose**
That rope is too <u>loose</u>.	**loose**
Is the knot in the string <u>loose</u>?	**loose**

piece *and* **peace:**

Take a <u>piece</u> of cake.	**piece**
Have you taken that <u>piece</u> of material?	**piece**
<u>Peace</u> was declared a year ago.	**peace**
There was a long period of <u>peace</u> in the country.	**peace**

to, too, two:

Sally went <u>to</u> the shop.	**to**
The boy ran <u>to</u> the village.	**to**
Sam went <u>too</u>.	**too**
She was <u>too</u> tired.	**too**
They had <u>two</u> books.	**two**
<u>Two</u> of the boys left early.	**two**

Other frequently misspelt words:

• She <u>always</u> completes the work.	**always**
• At the <u>beginning</u> of the day the weather was fine.	**beginning**
• He did not <u>believe</u> the worker.	**believe**
• She had a <u>bruise</u> on her leg.	**bruise**
• The <u>burglar</u> was captured.	**burglar**
• The woman bought a <u>business</u> in the city.	**business**
• The athlete completed the <u>circuit</u>.	**circuit**
• Has he <u>enough</u> fuel for the journey?	**enough**
• She left in <u>February</u>.	**February**
• They went into the <u>forest</u>.	**forest**
• The <u>fruit</u> was picked in the morning.	**fruit**
• Did she <u>guess</u> the answer?	**guess**

- They <u>heard</u> the loud sound.   **heard**
- The cliff rose to a great <u>height</u>.   **height**
- The injured man was taken to <u>hospital</u>.   **hospital**
- The <u>jewels</u> were in the case.   **jewels**
- I heard a <u>knock</u> on the door.   **knock**
- The orange <u>juice</u> was very fresh.   **juice**
- The book was returned to the <u>library</u>.   **library**
- The sound of the drill was a <u>nuisance</u>.   **nuisance**
- On this special <u>occasion</u> many people attended.   **occasion**
- The accident <u>occurred</u> at the intersection.   **occurred**
- The cakes were made with a special <u>recipe</u>.   **recipe**
- Do the words <u>rhyme</u>?   **rhyme**
- It was a <u>rough</u> track.   **rough**
- The man <u>says</u> that he can complete the work.   **says**
- It is a <u>straight</u> line.   **straight**
- There was some <u>trouble</u> in the town.   **trouble**
- The man was <u>truly</u> sorry.   **truly**
- She <u>used</u> to play tennis.   **used**
- They saw a <u>variety</u> of animals.   **variety**
- Here is the <u>woollen</u> cloth.   **woollen**
- The <u>whole</u> class went on the excursion.   **whole**
- The <u>yacht</u> was tied up at the pier.   **yacht**

SPELL-CHECK 6

After completing pages 99 to 103 try these two tests.

- Have someone read each sentence and repeat slowly the word underlined.
- Your task – write each word correctly.

6A. He <u>hasn't</u> been here.
<u>It's</u> a new car.
<u>You'd</u> like to see it.
They <u>shouldn't</u> go there.
<u>We're</u> leaving for our holidays.
<u>We'd</u> like to see you.
I <u>can't</u> finish this work.
<u>There's</u> a truck in the yard.
He <u>doesn't</u> enjoy the game.
I know <u>they'll</u> finish the work.
He <u>thought</u> he saw him.
She <u>taught</u> him to play the violin.
They walked <u>through</u> the bush.
Did he <u>receive</u> a present?
Have you been <u>there</u> before?

6B. Sue will <u>practise</u> the piano.
Can you <u>choose</u> a new book?
The car went <u>past</u> the park.
He <u>brought</u> the ball with him.
She had a <u>piece</u> of cake.
<u>Two</u> girls went to the show.
She went <u>to</u> the movies.
Did you <u>lose</u> the money?
She <u>always</u> does her work well.
Can you <u>guess</u> the answer.
Did you hear the <u>knock</u> on the door.
He went last <u>February</u>.
They took <u>enough</u> money with them.
The <u>fruit</u> is in the bowl.
The woman was sent to <u>hospital</u>.

> **Homophones are words that sound alike but are spelt differently.**

The <u>air</u> was fresh and clear.	**air**
The prince was <u>heir</u> to the throne.	**heir**
She was <u>allowed</u> to go.	**allowed**
They read the book <u>aloud</u>.	**aloud**
The boy <u>ate</u> the cake.	**ate**
She had <u>eight</u> books.	**eight**
They will <u>bail</u> water out of the boat.	**bail**
There is the <u>bale</u> of wool.	**bale**
His <u>bare</u> back was burnt by the sun.	**bare**
She could not <u>bear</u> to leave the dog.	**bear**
The <u>bean</u> crop was very good.	**bean**
He has <u>been</u> to the circus.	**been**
The <u>berry</u> was on top of the ice cream.	**berry**
They will <u>bury</u> the treasure.	**bury**
Fishermen brave the dangers of the Great Australian <u>Bight</u>.	**bight**
The dog will <u>bite</u> the other animal.	**bite**
The wind <u>blew</u> strongly.	**blew**
The shirt was a <u>blue</u> colour.	**blue**
Did you see the <u>boy</u>?	**boy**
The <u>buoy</u> was floating near the rocks.	**buoy**

brake	The <u>brake</u> on the bike did not work.
break	Did he <u>break</u> the ruler?
bread	They ate several slices of <u>bread</u>.
bred	The lions were <u>bred</u> in the zoo.
buy	We will <u>buy</u> the present.
by	He walked <u>by</u> the river.
bye	She will bid her friend good <u>bye</u>.
ceiling	They painted the <u>ceiling</u> in the kitchen.
sealing	The men were <u>sealing</u> up the old mine.
cent	He did not have a <u>cent</u>.
scent	The tracker dog followed the <u>scent</u>.
sent	She was <u>sent</u> away.
cereal	They had a bowl of <u>cereal</u>.
serial	I wrote down the <u>serial</u> numbers of the notes.
check	Did you <u>check</u> the work?
cheque	They wrote out a <u>cheque</u> for the goods.
chews	The animal <u>chews</u> on the bone.
choose	Will you <u>choose</u> a new book?
creak	The old timbers will <u>creak</u>.
creek	They went to the <u>creek</u>.
currant	The <u>currant</u> loaf was eaten.
current	There was a strong <u>current</u> in the creek.
dear	It was his <u>dear</u> friend.
deer	The <u>deer</u> was in the paddock.
desert	They travelled into the <u>desert</u>.
dessert	What will we have for <u>dessert</u>?
dew	The <u>dew</u> was on the grass.
due	The money is <u>due</u> to be paid today.

Many people <u>die</u> in wartime.	**die**
The red <u>dye</u> was very bright.	**dye**
She has <u>fair</u> hair.	**fair**
The <u>fare</u> on the bus was one dollar.	**fare**
His <u>feet</u> were sore after the long run.	**feet**
Crossing the desert was a great <u>feat</u>.	**feat**
They could not <u>find</u> the money.	**find**
The motorist was <u>fined</u> for speeding.	**fined**
This is a fine <u>fir</u> tree.	**fir**
The animal had grey <u>fur</u>.	**fur**
The <u>flour</u> was used to make the cake.	**flour**
He worked in the <u>flower</u> garden.	**flower**
She went <u>for</u> a walk.	**for**
There are <u>four</u> people at the shop.	**four**
The <u>fowl</u> was put in the shed.	**fowl**
It was a <u>foul</u> smell.	**foul**
The <u>grate</u> was made of iron.	**grate**
This is a <u>great</u> book.	**great**
I heard the <u>groan</u> of the injured pedestrian.	**groan**
She has <u>grown</u> a lot since last year.	**grown**
He <u>guessed</u> the answer.	**guessed**
She was a <u>guest</u> in the house.	**guest**
They danced in the <u>hall</u>.	**hall**
It was a large <u>haul</u> of fish.	**haul**
The wound will <u>heal</u>.	**heal**
The runner's left <u>heel</u> was blistered.	**heel**
Did you <u>hear</u> the sound?	**hear**
Come <u>here</u> at once!	**here**

herd	There is the <u>herd</u> of cattle.
heard	I <u>heard</u> the sound.
higher	This is <u>higher</u> than the ladder.
hire	Will you <u>hire</u> a car?
him	I saw <u>him</u> at the gate.
hymn	They sang a <u>hymn</u> at the service.
hoarse	The child was <u>hoarse</u> from shouting.
horse	The <u>horse</u> is in the paddock.
hole	There is a <u>hole</u> in the fence.
whole	Do not eat the <u>whole</u> cake?
hour	Meet me in one <u>hour</u>.
our	This is <u>our</u> new car.
knew	I <u>knew</u> the answer.
new	Where is the <u>new</u> boat?
knot	Tie the <u>knot</u> carefully.
not	She is <u>not</u> coming to the party.
know	He does not <u>know</u> where the car is.
no	She has <u>no</u> money.
knows	The boy <u>knows</u> the answer.
nose	The player injured his <u>nose</u>.
lead	The <u>lead</u> pipe is brand new.
led	They <u>led</u> the horse into the paddock.
loan	He had a <u>loan</u> of his friend's bike.
lone	The <u>lone</u> animal grazed in the field.
mail	She collected the <u>mail</u>.
male	A <u>male</u> tiger was in the ring.
main	They went along the <u>main</u> road.
mane	The lion had a golden <u>mane</u>.

They bought some <u>meat</u> for dinner.	**meat**
The girl will <u>meet</u> her at the bridge.	**meet**
She did not <u>mind</u> the noise.	**mind**
The workers <u>mined</u> for coal.	**mined**
The arrow <u>missed</u> the target.	**missed**
They could not see through the <u>mist</u>.	**mist**
She had a <u>pale</u> face.	**pale**
They carried a large <u>pail</u> of water.	**pail**
The <u>pain</u> in the injured arm was severe.	**pain**
The ball broke the <u>pane</u> of glass.	**pane**
She <u>passed</u> the slow moving vehicle.	**passed**
I walked <u>past</u> the yard.	**past**
There was a <u>pause</u> in the news broadcast.	**pause**
The kitten has tiny <u>paws</u>.	**paws**
The dog had an injured <u>paw</u>.	**paw**
<u>Pour</u> out the milk.	**pour**
The woman was in <u>poor</u> health.	**poor**
Late in the year <u>peace</u> was declared.	**peace**
Have a <u>piece</u> of cake?	**piece**
The animals wandered onto the <u>plain</u>.	**plain**
The <u>plane</u> landed in the swamp.	**plane**
The <u>rain</u> poured down.	**rain**
The country was settled in the <u>reign</u> of George III.	**reign**
Take the horse's <u>rein</u> please.	**rein**
This diamond is <u>real</u>.	**real**
He took his fishing <u>reel</u> with him.	**reel**
This is the <u>right</u> time to finish it.	**right**
Can he <u>write</u> the book?	**write**

road	The car travelled down the <u>road</u>.
rode	She <u>rode</u> the pony at the show.
sail	Can you <u>sail</u> this boat?
sale	The <u>sale</u> was on at the shopping centre.
saw	I <u>saw</u> the new sports car.
sore	The boy had a <u>sore</u> arm.
scene	It was a <u>scene</u> of great beauty.
seen	Have you <u>seen</u> the lost dog?
scent	The dog followed the <u>scent</u> of the lost boy.
sent	She was <u>sent</u> to collect the books.
sea	The <u>sea</u> was very calm.
see	Can you <u>see</u> that small shrub?
sew	They will <u>sew</u> the cloth.
sow	The farmer will <u>sow</u> the paddock.
so	It was <u>so</u> heavy he could not lift it.
some	They had <u>some</u> cake.
sum	She has a large <u>sum</u> of money.
stair	Climb that <u>stair</u> please.
stare	Do not <u>stare</u> at those people.
steal	They should not <u>steal</u> the money.
steel	She found the <u>steel</u> bar.
tail	The small pony has a long <u>tail</u>.
tale	They were told an interesting <u>tale</u>.
their	I saw <u>their</u> house.
there	<u>There</u> are many books on the shelves.
they're	<u>They're</u> going to the movies.
threw	She <u>threw</u> the ball at the fence.
through	The horse galloped <u>through</u> the scrub.

The ship was <u>tied</u> up at the wharf.	**tied**
The <u>tide</u> came in at six o'clock.	**tide**
I went <u>to</u> the shop.	**to**
Sam went <u>too</u>.	**too**
We bought <u>two</u> drinks.	**two**
The belt was round her <u>waist</u>.	**waist**
They did not <u>waste</u> any food.	**waste**
Sam will <u>wait</u> at the gate.	**wait**
The box was 10 kilograms in <u>weight</u>.	**weight**
The <u>war</u> was over at the end of the year.	**war**
She <u>wore</u> a pretty red dress.	**wore**
Did you <u>warn</u> them about the fire?	**warn**
His shoes were nearly <u>worn</u> out.	**worn**
The string was very <u>weak</u>.	**weak**
They will go home in a <u>week</u>.	**week**
I do not like this cold <u>weather</u>.	**weather**
She does not know <u>whether</u> or not to leave.	**whether**
Do you know <u>which</u> book to study?	**which**
The <u>witch</u> was a character in the story.	**witch**
<u>Who's</u> going to the movies?	**who's**
I do not know <u>whose</u> book this is?	**whose**
The young girl easily <u>won</u> the race.	**won**
<u>One</u> of the horses is missing.	**one**
The <u>wood</u> in the corner was rotting.	**wood**
She <u>would</u> not finish the work.	**would**

Your Own Spelling List

Write any words that you keep spelling incorrectly on this page.
Create a jingle for each word to help you remember the correct
spelling.

Look at the examples below:

separate has **a rat** in it.

independent has **three e's**.

definite is **finite**.

_____

_____

_____

_____

_____

_____

_____

_____

_____

_____

_____

_____

_____

_____

_____

_____

_____

8   1 ball 2 hat 3 key 4 table 5 five 6 pig 7 window
     8 jug 9 seven 10 ladder 11 mouse 12 dog 13 car
     14 orange 15 van 16 yacht 17 rain 18 nine 19 zebra
     20 apple 21 gate 22 elephant 23 ink 24 umbrella

9   1 flag 2 frog 3 drum 4 sled 5 smoke 6 skeleton
     7 shark 8 swim 9 snake 10 twelve 11 crab 12 glass
     13 truck 14 plant 15 grapes 16 stamp

10   1 spoon 2 blocks 3 pram 4 wheel 5 scorpion 6 chain
     7 broom 8 quarter 9 cloud 10 star 11 spring
     12 screw 13 splash 14 three 15 strawberry

12   1 bin 2 box 3 cap 4 cup 5 bus 6 bed

13   1 dog 2 fan 3 hut 4 gun 5 ham 6 log 7 kiss 8 nut
     9 leg 10 dam

14   1 rat 2 van 3 web 4 map 5 mop 6 hat 7 pen 8 sun
     9 cat 10 ten

15   1 big 2 dug 3 fin 4 lap

16   1 jut 2 mud 3 pet 4 rub 5 sag 6 top

17   1 mob 2 his 3 pan 4 sap 5 wig 6 keg

18   1 bin 2 fin 3 cat 4 bat 5 leg 6 beg 7 rat 8 sat

19   1 bag 2 beg 3 fan 4 fin 5 dog 6 dug 7 zip 8 zap

20   1 bin 2 bit 3 van 4 vat 5 bat 6 bag 7 leg 8 let

21   1 drill 2 shell 3 dress 4 flag 5 truck 6 crab

22   1 grass 2 twelve 3 bridge 4 stump 5 snow 6 screw
     7 grapes 8 stop 9 chess 10 cross

23   1 skid 2 blew 3 clap 4 smog

24   1 spun 2 glad 3 from 4 grab 5 shut 6 trap

25   1 scum 2 tram 3 prop 4 crag 5 brim 6 grim

32   A. 1 wage 2 shine 3 slate 4 plane 5 grime 6 hide
       7 ride 8 dine 9 dote 10 clothe
     B. All are yes

36   1 yes, no, yes; no, yes, yes
     2 snow – below, mellow, blow
       cow – foul, sound, how, amount, noun, howl, cowl
     3 pay – stay, clay, hay, bray, stray
       new – threw, clue, review, blue, chew

37 1 nd 2 sk 3 mp 4 lt 5 sh

38 1 le 2 ve 3 se 4 ce 5 ge

39 1 ing 2 ong 3 ang 4 ung 5 nch 6 tch

40 1 twice 2 stale or stole 3 chick or chock or chuck
4 shave or shove

41 1 grace 2 trace or truce 3 stage 4 brace
5 space or spice 6 crunch 7 snatch or snitch

43 1 back, pack, rack, lack, tack, stack
2 ran, can, than, scan, plan, span
3 well, sell, tell, shell, spell, smell
4 tall, call, fall, hall, stall, small

44 1 lake, take, make, snake, shake, drake
2 bark, mark, park, dark, spark, stark
3 late, hate, mate, skate, plate, crate
4 men, pen, den, when, then, hen
5 day, may, say, tray, stay, spray
6 hit, bit, fit, spit, flit, slit
7 get, met, wet, net, bet, fret

45 1 will, fill, kill, drill, frill, grill
2 not, got, lot, shot, plot, slot
3 fun, run, gun, spun, stun, shun
4 dig, rig, fig, jig, sprig, twig
5 win, fin, tin, thin, spin, shin
6 log, jog, hog, fog, slog, clog
7 low, mow, grow, show, slow, flow

46 1 same, game, tame, came, name, shame
2 made, fade, jade, trade, blade, spade
3 hike, like, pike, strike, spike, trike
4 look, took, cook, shook, crook, brook
5 tool, cool, fool, stool, school, spool
6 coat, goat, moat, float, gloat, throat
7 deep, peep, weep, sleep, steep, sweep

47 1 down, town, brown, frown, crown, drown
2 land, hand, stand, grand, brand, strand
3 few, new, crew, brew, blew, stew
4 fight, tight, might, slight, flight, fright
5 lick, sick, chick, trick, slick, thick
6 lump, bump, sump, thump, clump, slump
7 hide, side, tide, ride, slide, stride

48 1 pace, lace, race, grace, space, place
2 just, must, rust, dust, trust, thrust
3 punch, munch, bunch, hunch, brunch, crunch
4 damp, ramp, camp, stamp, cramp, champ
5 fed, led, red, sled, fled, bled
6 nod, sod, pod, rod, shod, plod
7 rag, tag, lag, wag, stag, crag

49 1 all, call, fall, hall, mall, small, stall, tall, thrall, wall
2 Ben, den, fen, hen, Ken, men, when, wren, yen
3 bog, clog, cog, fog, frog, hog, jog, log, smog
4 brook, cook, chook, crook, hook, look, nook, rook
5 bump, dumb, frump, grump, hump, jump, lump, pump

50 1 tug, rug, hug, snug, plug, slug
2 nut, cut, but, jut, shut, strut
3 ram, dam, jam, cram, gram, tram
4 rim, dim, brim, grim, trim, slim
5 hum, rum, gum, plum, glum, scum
6 map, nap, sap, trap, slap, strap
7 nip, hip, tip, ship, slip, strip

51 1 hop, mop, top, slop, shop, chop
2 jab, tab, cab, drab, stab, scab
3 sob, rob, job, blob, slob, throb
4 rub, hub, cub, grub, snub, shrub
5 deck, peck, check, fleck, speck, wreck
6 dock, rock, sock, stock, block, chock
7 luck, muck, suck, truck, stuck, struck

52 1 bend, mend, lend, fend, trend, blend
2 lent, bent, rent, went, dent, spent
3 hunt, runt, stunt, shunt, blunt, brunt
4 rest, pest, test, best, chest, crest
5 hint, tint, lint, glint, flint, print
6 hunk, junk, sunk, clunk, bunk, shrunk

53 1 gang, sang, hang, slang, clang, sprang
2 lung, rung, sung, stung, flung, strung
3 hush, lush, rush, crush, flush, plush
4 bank, rank, sank, spank, plank, shrank
5 dash, lash, sash, crash, clash, smash
6 catch, batch, latch, hatch, snatch, scratch
7 ditch, pitch, hitch, switch, twitch, stitch

ANSWERS SPELLING

115

54
1 heat, meat, treat, wheat, pleat, bleat
2 seen, keen, been, sheen, screen, green
3 ream, team, cream, steam, dream, scream
4 gain, pain, lain, plain, brain, strain
5 room, boom, loom, doom, gloom, groom
6 bail, pail, rail, frail, trail, snail
7 noon, soon, boon, croon, spoon, swoon

55
1 meet, sleet, greet, sweet, fleet, street
2 toil, boil, coil, foil, spoil, broil
3 raw, paw, law, draw, straw, claw
4 peek, reek, week, meek, cheek, sleek
5 bout, rout, spout, stout, scout, clout
6 need, reed, heed, seed, bleed, greed
7 weak, beak, leak, speak, bleak, streak

56
1 gum, hum, plum, rum, scum, sum, strum
2 bop, cop, chop, crop, drop, flop, hop, lop, mop, pop, plop, prop, shop, top
3 best, chest, crest, dressed, impressed, jest, lest, pest, rest, test, vest, west
4 attach, batch, catch, hatch, latch, patch, scratch, snatch
5 cub, club, dub, grub, hub, nub, rub, shrub, snub, stub

57
1 stink – pink or kink or link or rink
2 blend – mend or bend or tend or fend
3 trash – mash or hash or bash or lash or crash
4 slang – bang or tang or fang
5 trunk – bunk or junk or sunk or clunk

58
1 stand – band or hand or land
2 cling – ring or king
3 switch – itch or pitch
4 place – race or face or case
5 chink – ink or rink or flint or lint
6 stash – mash or cash or rash or bash
7 graft – raft or craft or aft.

59
1 broke, spoke, stroke 2 stale, whale, scale 3 thong, prong, strong 4 dart, chart, start 5 stove, grove, drove 6 spare, stare, scare 7 grace, space, trace 8 slope, grope, scope 9 hike, strike, spike

60   I lute, flute, brute. 2 cheer, steer, sneer. 3 loot, shoot, scoot. 4 bind, grind, blind. 5 grape, shape, scrape. 6 chair, flair, stair. 7 clear, shear, spear. 8 twine, spine, whine. 9 fable, gable, stable. 10 drive, strive, thrive. 11 swipe, tripe, stripe.

61   I cane, wane, lane. 2 snoop, troop, stoop. 3 crime, grime, prime. 4 stone, drone, prone. 5 slave, grave, shave. 6 those, chose, prose. 7 smile, while, mile. 8 moss, floss, gloss. 9 spark, shark, stark. 10 shook, crook, brook. 11 sought, brought, thought.

62   I shame – tame, lame, game. 2 stale – whale, tale, scale. 3 spark– park, bark, stark, mark. 4 blind – mind, bind, kind, hind. 5 grave – save, pave, rave, stave.

63   I skirt – dirt, shirt, flirt. 2 frame – tame, lame, came, dame. 3 flute – cute, lute, mute. 4 blink – link, kink, drink, think. 5 prong – long, strong, gong. 6 snatch – batch, latch, catch, match. 7 drift – lift, gift, sift, swift.

67   I k, k, k, k. 2 b, b, b, b.

68   I l, l, l, l. 2 g, g, g, g.

69   I h, h, h, h. 2 c, c, c, c. 3 w, w, w, w.

70   I flag, float, floor, flour, flake, flick, flash.
2 from, front, frost, free, frill, fruit, frown.
3 drop, draw, drug, drain, dream, drive, dress.
4 stain, state, starch, still, start, stone, story.

71   I space, speed, spoon, sport, spark, spend, spoke.
2 block, black, blind, blade, blood, blast, blank.
3 probe, pride, print, prowl, prime, prize, price.
4 what, when, while, whelk, white, whale, wheat.
5 scar, scare, scale, scarf, score, scoop, scout.
6 chat, chop, chill, check, chair, child, chart.

72   I quiet, quite, quick, quack, quake, quilt, quest.
2 crop, cramp, cross, crown, crowd, crash, crater.
3 glade, glad, glean, glass, globe, gleam, glance.
4 place, plane, plant, plush, plank, plead, plastic.
5 truce, trade, train, tribe, tried, trust, trash.
6 green, great, grant, group, ground, grain, grasp.

ANSWERS SPELLING

117

ANSWERS SPELLING

73 1 small, smart, smash, smell, smile, smack, smooth.
2 skip, skin, skunk, skill, skirt, skate, sketch.
3 shell, shoes, shiny, shave, shore, shoot, shape.
4 swim, sway, sweet, sweep, swift, swipe, swamp.
5 snap, snag, snack, snarl, snake, sneak, snatch.
6 twin, twice, twist, tweak, tweet, tweed, twitch.

74 1 bread, break, bring, broke, broom, brown, breeze.
2 clay, clip, clock, class, close, climb, clothes.
3 sprain, spray, spread, sprint, sprinkle.
4 scrum, scrub, scrape, scratch, scraps.
5 splash, splice, splint, split, splotch.
6 street, strand, string, stream, stroke.

75 1 start, state. 2 spoke, spend. 3 while, wheat.
4 check, child.

76 1 crash, crowd. 2 trust, trash. 3 group, grasp. 4 shiny,
shoot. 5 snarl, snatch. 6 broke, breeze. 7 clock, class.

82 A. 1 crosses 2 taxes 3 girls 4 daisies 5 circuses
6 loaves 7 lions 8 launches 9 beaches 10 lives
11 lollies 12 photos 13 wishes 14 buses 15 whales
16 thieves 17 sheep 18 journeys 19 jerseys
20 echoes
B. 1 factories 2 injuries 3 ladies 4 berries 5 valleys
6 jockeys 7 relays 8 gullies 9 memories 10 buoys
11 armies 12 cities.

84 1 cooked 2 tricked 3 entering 4 smiled 5 planned
6 ripping 7 spied 8 shaped 9 hoping 10 worried.

85 1 howls, howled, howling. 2 jokes, joked, joking.
3 drips, dripped, dripping. 4 replies, replied, replying.
5 smiles, smiled, smiling. 6 places, placed, placing.
7 rests, rested, resting. 8 enters, entered, entering.
9 walks, walked, walking. 10 loads, loaded, loading.
11 rips, ripped, ripping. 12 dries, dried, drying.

88 enrich, midnight, uphill, reduce, exclaim, underneath,
conduct, overpay, project, unclean, outlay, insane,
prefer, decay, subway, forecast.

90 hope<u>less</u>, paint<u>er</u>, streng<u>th</u>, care<u>ful</u>, brother<u>hood</u>, drink<u>able</u>, pol<u>ish</u>, refug<u>ee</u>, wood<u>en</u>, simplif<u>y</u>, silk<u>en</u>, act<u>or</u>, enjoy<u>ment</u>, peril<u>ous</u>, art<u>ist</u>, length<u>en</u>, leg<u>al</u>, act<u>ion</u>, manage<u>ment</u>, bak<u>er</u>.

91 1 skip per, com mon, traf fic, hid den
2 pet rol, cac tus, is land, pic nic
3 sig nal, trac tor, bul let, but ton
4 whis per, ber ry, writ ten, thun der
5 com pan y, frag ment, es cape, cot tage
6 buf fa lo, mat ter, tun nel, an vil
7 ar tis tic, cir cum vent.

92 1 na tion, clo ver, o cean, la dies
2 pi per, pi rate, na tive sto ker
3 lu nar, re gion, fe male, a gent
4 cu bic, lo cal, e rase, ru ler

93 A. 1 prin cess, ex claim, ail ment, fab ric
2 im por tant, win ter, ber ries, cap tive
3 fre quent, do main, rat tle, cra dle
4 o cean, na tion, vi brate, jas mine
B. 1 yes, yes, no, yes.
2 yes, yes, no, no.
3 yes, no, yes, yes.
4 yes, no, no, yes.
C. 1 cur tain 2 cas tle 3 can dle 4 mon key.
D. 1 in cred i ble, pro fes sor, im por tant, fan tas tic
2 hos pi tal i ty, stu dy ing, un ea si ness, con tent ment
3 un oc cu pied, ex cep tion, sin gu lar, con trac tions.

95 1 firefly 2 footpath 3 goldfish 4 drumstick 5 sunlight
6 rainfall 7 logbook 8 rainbow 9 watchdog
10 paintbrush

96 A. 1 himself, anything, goodbye, overhead, bulldozer.
2 jackknife, pineapple, myself, seaside, homewards.
3 township, upstairs, halfway, patchwork, campfire.
B. 1 fingernail 2 horseshoe 3 Answers will vary

99 1 she's 2 we'd 3 they've 4 she'll 5 that's 6 you're

Copyright © 1996 P Walker
Reprinted 2002, 2003, 2005, 2006, 2007 (twice), 2008, 2010 (twice)

ISBN 978 1 86441 061 7

Pascal Press
PO Box 250
Glebe NSW 2037
(02) 8585 4044
www.pascalpress.com.au

Designed by Love of Design
Typesetting by Artribute
Printed by Green Giant Press